◇◇◇◇◇◇◇◇◇

SUMMER SOLSTICE

◇◇◇◇◇◇◇◇◇

SUMMER SOLSTICE

AN ESSAY

Nina MacLaughlin

BLACK SPARROW PRESS

BOSTON

Published in 2020 by BLACK SPARROW PRESS

GODINE
Boston, Massachusetts
godine.com

The four-part essay originally ran, in a slightly different form,
online at *The Paris Review Daily*.

LIBRARY OF CONGRESS CATALOGING–IN–PUBLICATION DATA
Names: MacLaughlin, Nina, author.
Title: Summer solstice : an essay / Nina MacLaughlin.
Description: Boston : Black Sparrow Press, 2020.
Identifiers: LCCN 2019056172 | ISBN 9781574232387 (paperback)
| ISBN 9781574232394 (ebook)
Subjects: LCSH: Summer. | Summer solstice.
Classification: LCC PS509.S87 M33 2020 | DDC 813/.6--dc23
LC record available at https://lccn.loc.gov/2019056172

SECOND PRINTING, 2023
Printed in The United States of America

Contents

The Start of Summer

I T WAS early June, Saturday, midmorning on the Red Line. I was moving through tunnels beneath Cambridge when a teenager approached and asked if I wanted to take part in a memory project. Take an index card and a pen and write down a memory, any memory at all, and get one from a stranger in return. I took a card, a pen, and wrote. I handed it to her, and before we reached the next stop she returned and handed me a memory that belonged to another person on the subway car. It was written on an index card folded in half:

> On the last night of summer camp, my best
> friends and I snuck out of our cabins and slept
> on the tennis courts so we could stargaze
> and spoon with each other all night. I saw 6
> shooting stars that night.

Such is summer. Unroofed, under stars, away from parents, away from rules, pressing against friends, laughing, urgent whispers—*did you hear that?*—quiet,

quiet, earth as bed and sky as blanket. The stars sweep across the sky in silence, heaven's hemispheric map-makers, time-tellers, their positions revealing where in the year we are.

Where in the year are we? We don't need to track the stars to know. Here in the northern hemisphere, each evening's longer light alerts us. Right now the year is skipping toward the opening of the heated season. Which, for some, begins on the First of June. Where you define the start of the summer depends on whether you align yourself with the meteorological calendar, which is used by climatologists and meteorologists, or the astronomical calendar. If you stand with the scientists, June 1 starts summer (and September 1 starts fall, December 1, winter, and March 1, spring). If you base your seasonal switches on the earth's tilt and changing relationship to the sun, the solstice opens the season, falling always between June 20 and June 22, when, in the northern hemisphere, the sun reaches its highest point in the sky and light lasts longer than any other day of the year.

We're getting there. Here in this small city in the northeastern United States where I write from, on the First of June, the sun will rise at 5:10 AM and set at 8:14 at night, which is one minute and seventeen seconds longer than the day before. For a stretch of seventeen days in March, daylight lengthens by two minutes and fifty-two seconds every day. That's close to fifty minutes more daylight in just over two weeks.

March is one of my least favorite months. Too much flat, pale light all at once. Now's different. "June was white," writes Virginia Woolf in *The Waves*. "I see the fields white with daisies, and white with dresses; and tennis courts marked with white. Then there was wind and violent thunder. There was a star riding through clouds one night, and I said to the star, 'Consume me.'" What else can you say to a star?

Long light and there's something in the air. Frog-song and bug-song in the air. Honeysuckle in the air. Dew in the air and beading on the tips of petal tongues. Soon, maybe, campfire smoke in the shoulder of the sweatshirt of the person lying next to you on the tennis court, in their hair, smoke in their hair. And now and then, above, a whisking line of light across the darkness, evanescent, effervescent as a soda bubble at the back of the nose—*did you see that?*—there, gone, perception at the edge of the senses, a wish, and it is summer and there is freedom, and time, and luck to be had.

What's the start of summer for you, the signal that it's here? Is it the last day of school? The lilacs or day lilies? First sleep with the windows open? Smell of cut grass behind the gasoline of the lawn mower? The fat red tomato sliced thin and salted? A sunburn? Shins sweating? The first swim? The first hot dog off the grill? Throbbing light from the fireflies? Campfire smoke in your hair? Is it the first day of June? Is it the day when light's longest? When your midday shadow's shorter than any other day? When the sun sets and sets and sets?

In summer we tend skyward. It invites us out and up. We no longer hunch against the cold. We can stand outside when it's dark and lift our faces to the sky and get spun back to childhood or swung into the swishing infinity above. Aimee Nezhukumata-thil turns her eyes upward in her poem "Summer Haibun":

> There are not enough jam jars to can this
> summer sky at night. I want to spread those
> little meteors on a hunk of still-warm bread this
> winter. Any trace left on the knife will make a
> kitchen sink like that evening air
>
> the cool night before
> star showers: so sticky so
> warm so full of light

The grandfather of someone I knew filled ice trays with pesto made from the basil in his garden so that in the cold crust of winter he could pull a tray out from the freeze, twist out a green-black cube, soften it with heat, and return to sitting shirtless at the table on the patio, limbs loosened. The buttery warmth, harvested and jarred, and spread on bread in winter. There's warmth enough to look up when the sun's down. And the sense, in summer, that there's time enough to do so, too, time enough for all of it, in a languid, damp, and heat-fuzzed way. An atmosphere of, I'll get to it but right now, a beer before dinner and warmth on bare legs, and everything can just go a little slower for a moment. The light lasts forever, life lasts forever. Do you feel young? *I promise*, the start of summer whispers, *you are young*.

Summer strums the loose low chords of freedom and release. Feel it in the space between your shoulders. It's the nostalgic season, arriving all warm-breezed and verdant, putting its heavy arm around you and whispering, *Come on, come on, remember?* Let's return to the screen door slamming, bare feet on the porch floor, peach juice sticky on the chin, sun on the back of your neck. You can return to a time of more time. Summer brings the memory of summer, a gentle flight backward. It's the season when a person can feel their wingspan again.

At a museum in Salem, Massachusetts, taxidermied birds behind glass cases line a wall; who knows when they last launched themselves off land and moved through air spread-winged in flight. Nearby, an interactive wind display—move the small steering wheel, see the way the movement of air shifts the fine white sand. The height of the wheel prescribes the age of those interacting with it. One afternoon, a toddler, three feet high, in checkered overalls, twisted the wheel this way, that, back-forth, and the fan inside flung the sand into rippled dunes. The toddler's father crouched behind him and spoke quietly in the small boy's ear. "See it move?" he said. "You're doing that."

In "Jet," Tony Hoagland moves upward into the air and sky, writing of being on the back porch with beers and friends; they "soar up into the summer stars. / Summer. The big sky river rushes overhead, / bearing asteroids and mist, blind fish / and old space suits with skeletons inside." The skeletons collect and the summer sky at night brings him forward and back.

> We gaze into the night
> as if remembering the bright unbroken planet
> we once came from,
> to which we will never
> be permitted to return.
> We are amazed how hurt we are.
> We would give anything for what we have.

Summer whispers away, making promises about returning to that unbroken planet—is it youth, maybe? Or further back, the muggy warmth of the womb? Or is it the pre-broken planet of our own cracked and divided selves? Is there any going back? Only by way of the green-hedged memories of what was. But what's the harm in trusting summer's lull for a night or two? Release yourself into the sky and feel, for a moment: there's time. The faded smell of grill smoke and sunscreen in the air. The buttery spread of stars in the air. The oak leaves touching oak leaves on branches in the air. We have the rest of the year to hurry, to feel time's press, to be nagged by the feeling of a promise unkept. We start summer as we end: empty-handed, trying to steer the wind.

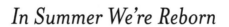

In Summer We're Reborn

W E START in the stars and move to the womb, which is to say water, which is to say swimming, which is the best part of summer.

We'll ease in. On the dawn of the summer solstice, rouse yourself from bed and head to the lawn or the field or the garden, kneel in the grass or the mulch, and with palms open, touch the grass or leaves or petals, get the damp on your hands, and put the wetness to your face. Power lives in the solstice dew—it gives youth, beauty, health, new glow. Especially true for maidens, it's said, but all can take part. Take a dew bath in the solstice dawn. It makes sense somehow with the residual self-evidence of childhood—oh, of course the solstice dew holds magic—like a belief in fairies or demons. There's a lot in this world we can't see.

Dew is the damp left behind as day is born out of night, "a child of moon and air," according to the lyric poet Alkman, writing in the seventh century B.C. Air and moon mingle and the result is a bead on the grass blade. Haikuist Kobayashi Issa writes:

The world of dew
is the world of dew.
And yet, and yet—

Here, the dash is the haiku's Rorschach test—how
does your brain fill in what's next? This world is real,
but it won't last long. This world exists and yet—we
can't enter it, and yet—we live right in it. And yet
the world of dew is not a world at all. And yet what is
a world and what are we doing? What now? On the
solstice, a baptism with these beads brings renewal,
purification, a whole new life. We're made fresh and
ready. When Christianity took sway over paganism,
there came a midsummer day, the midpoint between
planting and harvest, known as Saint John's Eve. It
marks the feast day of Saint John the Baptist, he who
dipped people in the river and washed them of their
sin, he who rebirthed people in the water.

There's a river in Eastern Europe. Imagine yourself on the shore, holding a crown you've made of
flowers, and imagine the person you love, or desire,
or feel curious to kiss, is on the other side of the
river with crowds of people. You are with crowds of
people on your side of the shore, and you place the
crown onto the water and watch it float across the
river to see who receives it on the other side. Imagine
your hope that it's the one person you want. Flowers
floating across the river to see if you find good luck

in love—this is another solstice tradition, another upping of the chances that love—and new lives—might be born.

Summer's when the world gets born again. Tove Jansson, in *The Summer Book*, a novel luminous as a piece of beach glass, writes about a grandmother and granddaughter who live together on an island in Norway, and of the midsummer celebrations there. The granddaughter starts the day stormy, and the grandmother longs to tell her, "I understand how awful it is here. Here you come, headlong into a tight little group of people who have always lived together, who have the habit of moving around each other on land they know and own and understand." She's talking about arriving on the island, but she might as well be talking about arriving into life, the violent expelling from our original swim, our unprotected entry, wholly vulnerable, into a clutch of others who've been around, who have their habits, ways, and limits. Everything, even breath, is new.

Swimming offers an approximation of reentry. Is it possible to enter a body of water and not emerge altered in some way? Even to get rained on can change the vibration of an afternoon. In water, one can surrender oneself in a way not possible on a hill, or canyon, or dune. What I like best is giving my weight to it, the possibility of being held and the possibility of drowning.

A summer evening a few years ago, I sat by a lake with a friend and we talked about bodies of water. My friend likes lakes because you can see all the edges. Too much infinity with the ocean, which is just why I like it. Edgeless, endless, there's a far shore somewhere but the in-between is incomprehensible. "Lakes are creepy," writes Heidi Julavits. "Where do the dead things go? This is why people are buried at sea but never at lake. The sea is a clean vanisher. A lake is a morgue."

I like to swim at Walden Pond. If you stand still, water up to your ankles, the small fishes come and bite at your toes. The water is clear, feels clean, gets deep. At the start of a summer, I went with a man who didn't know how to swim. He sat on a rock with his feet in the water and the small fishes came and bit on his toes. I went waist-deep. "I can help you," I said. "It feels so good. I can teach you how to swim." A ridiculous proposal because I can barely swim myself. I was not the first to make this offer to him. He declined and the sun warmed his shoulders.

I swam a short distance away from the shore; the water was quickly over my head. A residual pleasure from childhood is dropping myself to the bottom and then using the strong muscles in my legs to blast up through the surface. I sent my body downward. Down, down, where's the bottom, will I reach it, bubbles rising my body dropping, darker, colder.

And then the landing. I felt the sand with my feet and let my body hang there for a moment, suspended near the bottom, let every muscle dissolve, a total floating stillness, the front of my body aimed upward. I am gone. The world is gone. Everyone is gone. I have both entered and exited, and now the simplicity of hanging in space, held by the tiny silky hands of the water. Above, far away as the moon, gauzy light at the surface, shaking. I placed my feet on the sand, crouched, and with all the strength in my legs, pressed against the bottom and went rocketing up toward the light. I blasted through the surface, sucking air into my lungs. Had I been gone ten seconds? An hour? A year? In the moments I was out of existence, nothing had changed, and everything felt new.

I like that pond, but I like the ocean more.

Some summers ago, I was with two men at a beach. One on a towel on the sand, one in the waves with me. The waves were big and strong and moved us. I leapt into them, jumped, was pressed, let myself fall all the way underwater. They pushed me toward land and pulled me to sea. I dove through the tallest ones, my hair moved all down my back and I was stilled, suspended parallel to earth and sky. It felt good. I laughed, even in the danger (the waves were strong, and I am not a strong swimmer). The moon was nearing full, the waves were sucked toward its faraway white weight, higher, swelling,

stronger. They bashed, we let ourselves be knocked
around. I like the way May Swenson puts it in her
poem "Swimmers":

Tossed
by the muscular sea,
we are lost,
and glad to be lost
in troughs of rough
love.

There was love then. Earlier in the day, the man in
the waves and I had buried a geode in the yard as a
marriage pact. That night, around a table, we'd made
a toast to love. And that afternoon in the ocean, leaping like a child, I wondered: Have I ever been this
happy?

Tidal or still, river or pool, spangling bright blue
in the backyard, summer water pulls us in. "The
swimmer lets himself fall out of the day heat and
down through a gold bath of light deepening and
cooling into thousands of evenings, thousands of Au-
gusts, thousands of human sleeps," writes Anne Carson in *Plainwater*. It's an abandonment of thought, of
language, of self, through which we emerge whole.
A dissolution occurs akin to entering another's body
during sex, not in the simple penetrative sense, but
in the dissolving of boundaries between bones and
skin. The best fucks leave us not turned to stone, but

liquefied. In both water and sex, getting carried away is the point. Carson writes, "How slow is the slow trance of wisdom, which the swimmer swims into."

We enter water and we leave ourselves. Gravity loosens and we swim into a slow trance, we swim into wisdom. And what is the wisdom? It is of being un-separate. It is a temporary return to the unbroken planet, where we exist as both whole and dissolved. In the dark-bright of water, we're wet at the throat, at the back of the neck, in the ears, on the eyelids, and the water on the skin gives a literal cleansing. We emerge, from waves onto beach, up the shining metal ladder off the side of a pool, onto the twiggy banks of a river, onto a lakeshore surrounded by pine forest, first smoke of campfires rising on the banks, and the world is reset. We return to our selves, separate and distinct once again, severed from the All, with only the memory of that quick glimpse into the mystery of what was.

In her piece on swimming in a lake, Julavits writes of the bright green algae on the surface, and how the best thing about the swim was taking off her bathing suit to find that "the crotch was bright green . . . It was like getting my period for the first time and seeing the shock of color where normally there is only white." Summer is the saturated season. The color floods back in. Each dip is another shot at being reborn, into summer where the world's blood runs green.

Fecund Sounds Like a Swear

THE DELIGHTS of summer are earthly. An older friend lives for pleasure. Just north of sixty, with a thin ponytail and a thick mustache, he does seasonal work, landscaping, collects unemployment in the winter, and pursues the perfect high. After a knee injury, beers and hallucinogens gave way to pain pills. "I'll die of terminal boyhood," he tells me.

Another friend floods me with her schedule, her work, her workouts, this kid at soccer practice, that kid at gymnastics, the new dog needs walking, the groceries do not buy themselves, sixty hours at her job, thirty in her car to-ing and fro-ing. "Usually I've reached over ten-thousand steps by seven in the morning," she tells me.

When we were in high school, in fits over too much homework, one teacher would stop us mid-whine: "Complaining or bragging?" he'd ask. It's a question that comes to my mind when my friend enumerates her obligations. Complaining or bragging? It's a question I try to ask myself at certain moments, too. Is it bad, or are you proud? Is it bad, or do you want others to know what you're capable of? Is it bad, or is this how you identify yourself? How much does the toil define your life on earth? Now: It's summer. Time to take a load off for once. The wheel of the year is rolling toward the longest day, a breather, a pause. We're midway between the planting and the harvest, and it's time for the earth—soil, rain, and sun—to do its work. Can you take a rest? Can you aim yourself toward pleasure? Or are your work and life too intertwined? In other words, are you the grasshopper or are you the ant?

The fable has it this way: The grasshopper parties, plays music, brings joy to the other bugs. He dances the summer away. The ant toils, tunnels, lugs crumbs. He readies himself for winter. Come late fall, the grasshopper asks the ant for aid, and the go-getter scoffs and says, *You should've been working.* James Joyce puts it like this in *Finnegans Wake*: "The silly-billy of a Gracehoper had jingled through a jungle of love and debts and jangled through a jumble of life in doubts afterworse, wetting with the bimblebeaks, drikking with nautonects, bilking with durrydung-lecks and horing after ladybirdies." Nice life. Meanwhile, "His Gross the Ondt, prostrandvorous upon his dhrone, in his Papylonian babooshkees, smolking a spatial brunt of Hosana cigals, with unshrinkables farfalling from his unthinkables, swarming of himself in his sunnyroom," which doesn't sound so bad either, but it's a little hard to tell. The truth is this: "These twain are the twins that tick Homo Vulgaris."

The pleasure-seeking id, a seething sack holding all the hungers, the throbbing force of *now*, and the naysaying superego, severe and unremitting punisher, a strangling force that cinches closed the seething sack hissing *you should be ashamed.* Twin forces within us that tick back and forth as the ego tries to referee. Nathaniel Hawthorne's story "The May-Pole of Merry Mount" also reckons with this duality.

Quick history: Thomas Morton, lawyer, businessman, free spirit, crossed the seas from England in 1624 and settled in what would become Quincy, Massachusetts, having brought with him an attitude of no parents, no rules. Disdainful of the pleasure-denying Puritans, that dour lot of naysayers, he formed a colony with Captain Richard Wollaston, but split with him after finding out Wollaston had been selling indentured servants into slavery. Morton set up his own colony, Merry Mount, a utopian scenario, a realm with fewer strictures—revelry, debauch, peaceful intermingling with the Algonquin Indians. He set up a maypole, that pagan, pine tree phallus that rises ribboned to the sky, often in play during midsummer and summer solstice celebrations in northern Europe, and celebrated with settlers and Indians alike. The Puritans disapproved, particularly of the practice of marrying Indian brides. Governor

William Bradford was disgusted by the "beastly practices of ye mad Bacchanalians." Hawthorne captures the vibe: On the summer solstice, a wild crew gathers around the Merry Mount maypole. Among them, a young man with "the head and branching antlers of a stag"; another with "the grim visage of a wolf"; another with "the beard and horns of a venerable he-goat." Another looked like a bear, besides its pink silk stockings. And a real bear from the forest is in attendance as well, "as ready for the dance as any in that circle." They're governed by a "wild philosophy of pleasure:"

> Had a wanderer, bewildered in the melancholy forest, heard their mirth, and stolen a half-affrighted glance, he might have fancied them the crew of Comus, some already transformed to brutes, some midway between man and beast, and the other rioting in the flow of tipsy jollity that foreran the change.

It's a fertility fest: flowers, spinning ribbons, blooming love, lovemaking. The boundaries dissolve and we're drawn by waist-down forces. We're on earth alive, fleshed and smelling petals, grass, and fire smoke. Time does not get any longer than this, and fecund sounds like a swear. In Hawthorne's story, love gets celebrated, and a young man and maiden are there to be wed. But a band of Puritans, "most dismal wretches," lurk on the outskirts and spy on the scene. Hawthorne describes their life-denying work ethic, how they prayed in the morning, worked until evening, prayed again. "Their festivals were fast days . . . Woe to the youth or maiden who did but dream of a dance!"

The Puritans approach the seething midsummer celebration as "when waking thoughts start up amid the scattered fantasies of a dream." The punishers versus the pleasure-seekers, superego versus id, swarming ants versus fiddling grasshoppers. Hawthorne details what's at stake:

> The future complexion of New England was involved in this important quarrel. Should the grizzly saints establish their jurisdiction over the gay sinners, then would their spirits darken all the clime, and make it a land of clouded visages, of hard toil, of sermon and psalm forever. But should the banner staff of Merry Mount be fortunate, sunshine would break up on the hills, and flowers would beautify the forest, and late posterity do homage to the May-Pole.

In history, the Puritans considered Morton such a threat that they kicked him out of the country. He returned after a time, and when he did, he found his Indian friends dead from plague. He was arrested again, banished, and the Puritans burned Merry Mount to the ground. Look at the complexion of New England, look at the complexion of the United States: a land of clouded visages, a land that prizes toil, a land that espouses freedom, freedom, freedom—say what you want, marry who you want, pursue your own version of happiness—and yet, and yet—

"The most unfree souls go west, and shout of freedom," writes D. H. Lawrence, who claims we are "freest when we are most unconscious of freedom." Can we feel unconscious of freedom in the United States? Can we be unconscious of it when we are always supposed to, above all, be so conscious of it? Unfree souls go west, moving toward the setting sun, which these nights sets and sets and sets. Led Zeppelin knew: "There's a feeling I get when I look to the west and my spirit is crying for leaving." And Lawrence observes that "Americans have always been at a certain tension. Their liberty is a thing of sheer will, sheer tension: a liberty of THOU SHALT NOT. And it has been so from the first. The land of THOU SHALT NOT."

Land of the free, home of the ants. And the tension's tighter this time of year. Yes, there's license, yes, there's freedom, yes, there's drink and rest and sex. But the days are about to start getting shorter. Have you prepared for winter? Have you prepared to die? Can you really relax when there is so much left to do and what's approaching is more and more darkness?

Let's escape the shalt and shalt not. Let's dissolve the tension for just one minute. If you want, find a boy with a beautiful mouth to kiss you, pull flowers from the ground and weave them into a crown, escape to the shadows of the woods, forget yourself with someone else, pine needles in your hair, twigs pressed into the meat of your back, dirt against your heels as you thrash, under the trees with the animals, under the stars with the trees. Everything is swelling, blooming, glowing, all about to burst, fertile, verdant, ready, wet. It's summer! We will never have more time than we have now.

Summer Is Made of
the Memory of Summer

NEW SEASON. New you. We began in the sky, in the stardust, we moved wombward into the water, out into the earthly world, and we arrive, now, in fire. Happy first day of summer.

The solstice is a special day, irregular, when doors swing open that are otherwise closed, like on Halloween, like the winter solstice and the equinoxes. There are extra layers of possibility afoot. Open yourself, why not, ease yourself toward a more primal state of mind. A battle's taking place. Twins wage war for rulership over the year. According to the ancient myths, the Oak King has been in power since the solstice in December. For the six months of the year that light gets longer, he drops his acorns, spreads his seed, towers over much of the forest, embodying strength, potency, fertility. Now, after half a year at the helm, he's sapped. Today, the summer solstice, when the sun reaches its highest point in the sky here in the northern hemisphere, the Holly King, the dark mischievous other half, beats his brother, and takes the throne for the darkening part of the year. He'll rule through Yule.

The wheel of the year goes round—round like wreaths hung on doors in winter, round like flower crowns made in summer. Two halves within the whole, each force in tension with the other, pushing against, pulling apart, each wanting to overpower its opposite, its irreconcilable twin. "The very value attached to the life of the man-god necessitates his violent death as the only means of preserving it from the inevitable decay of age," writes James Frazer in *The Golden Bough*. "The same reasoning would apply to the King of the Wood; he, too, had to be killed in order that the divine spirit, incarnate in him, might be transferred in its integrity to his successor." Ritual death, a fertility fest, rebirth. Power rising, taking hold, falling, taking new form. "He must increase, but I must decrease," says John the Baptist of Jesus, born six months, a year's half-turn, before him. "You can never have a new thing without breaking an old," says D. H. Lawrence. "The new thing is the death of the old." What's coming?

We're wading in dualisms: heaven and hell, summer and winter, light and dark, ant and grass-hopper, holly and oak, superego and id, and—the big one—life and death, the circle whose warm-cool palms cup us all. See how Inger Christensen puts it in her book *it*:

The summer worn thin that comes back again and again, the summer laid waste that saves up for its next lavish coming, the pollen-dusted summer that rises from the dust, makes death immortal . . . A summer defined as winter. Wearing a mask. Playing its game to the end, its double game. In a color-rich duel with itself. Wearing its green cape casually over both shoulders, ready to look like a summer. And repeating: Summer is dead, summer might as well leaf out. Send out its fresh shoots once more to attain full, lush expression, repeat the flourishing decay.

We save up, we try to return, we prepare again and again for our next lavish coming, while the fact at the bottom is that every day it darkens. Darkness unspools so slowly it looks like light. The end unspools so slowly it seems like the start. Winter and summer—flowers and snow, holly and oak—dance with each other as they battle. Each is both at once. Our life means our death.

What's here, where we're standing, in the center? In plants and trees there is what's called the meristem, a collection of undifferentiated cells that maintain the capacity to proliferate throughout the entire life span of the plant. It's why trees keep growing, thicker and taller, through the years. Meristem. Merry stem. It might as well be another name for the maypole, the grand erection of the trunk, its penetration up and into the sky, ribboned approximation of the earth's axis. Meristem, this cellular force, this botanical meat or marrow, this pure child that exists in our full-fledged adulthood, obscured by layers of growth and knowing. As potter M. C. Richards writes in her book *Centering*, "Even at the top of the oldest oak there is the meristem, out which new leaves push. Child in man." It doesn't go away.

Oak often fed the bonfires on the summer solstice, according to Robert Graves in his book *The White Goddess*, which captivated Sylvia Plath. He calls midsummer an orgy of marriage and death. Throughout Europe, throughout history, bonfires blazed on the solstice, on hills and shores, on village streets, on riverbanks, in fields. The sun's retreating now, so let's make light last a little longer. Let's kindle our own small suns here on earth. People leapt over the flames, tossed their flower crowns into the flames, hoped their crops would rise to the height of the flames. In some places, couples leaping over the fire together would have good luck in fertility and love; elsewhere, the leap meant avoiding backache during the harvest. In Norway, the fire kept the cattle healthy and steered away the witches (they fly tonight). "At that mystic season the mountains open and from their cavernous depths the uncanny crew pours forth to dance and disport themselves for a time," writes Frazer.

On the summer solstice, the light lasts and lasts.

Here, in this small city in the Northeast, sundown happens at 8:24 that night, with one second more daylight than the day before. The next day will be two seconds shorter. The midsummer bonfires blaze and glow, and the shadows dance, dark wisps that sweep and fling themselves across the ground, against a mountainside, slipping between the trees, silent as the shooting stars. The fire fades, shadows swell and lengthen, get absorbed into the fuller dark. The uncanny crew slips back into the mountain fissures, and the hard oak burns to black ash. "Light though thou be, thou leapest out of darkness," raves Captain Ahab in *Moby-Dick*, "but I am darkness leaping out of light, leaping out of thee!" The fire glows, the shadows dance.

The fire rises. It's getting hotter. Time's the fire. It burns us new, it licks us clean, it consumes us all. Nothing is left uneaten.

The more you give the fire, the more it takes.

"Time is our ordeal," writes Richards, our trial by fire. She goes on: "Fire has its slow motion, its flare. Tedium, alarm, necessity. I tell you we are in it. The voice at the center speaks in tongues of flame." Here we are, finally, at the center. But we douse that voice with water, we try to extinguish those tongues of flame. We're scared of the fire, scared of what those tongues of flame will say. The truth at the center is white-hot and terrifying. What do we hear when we listen? What is revealed?

Beyond the fire some fifth element emerges. Call

it center, meristem, soul. "IT," Lawrence calls it, "the deepest *whole* self of man," the force we're driven by. "If we are living people, in touch with the source, IT drives us and decides us. We are free only so long as we obey." Access to IT liberates us as long as we follow where it leads. As long as we listen. We've got to be in touch with the source. How do we get there? Octavio Paz makes a map. From a section of the long poem *Sunstone*, which I taped to my wall behind my bedside table when I was sixteen years old and memorized:

> two bodies, naked and entwined,
> leap over time, they are invulnerable,
> nothing can touch them, they return to the source,
> there is no you, no I, no tomorrow,
> no yesterday, no names, the truth of two
> in a single body, a single soul,
> oh total being. . .

Leaping over time, leaping over flames, two as one, joined, joining, the slipping into the great whole. Part of reaching IT involves bypassing the black-and-white divisions, being awake to the paradoxical one-ness of it all. "The fight for freedom goes on. It is built in," writes Richards. The child in woman and man, the meristem, the force from the start.

"Summertime, time, time, Child, the livin's easy," Janis Joplin interpreted Gershwin's lyrics. "One of these mornings . . . you're gonna spread your wings, Child, and take, take to the sky." But until that morning, the song goes on, don't you cry. After that morning, who knows what harm may come. But for now, for now, the livin's easy. Tan lines. Hot dogs. The memory-fantasy of summer lives on. The world of dew is the world of dew, and yet, and yet. The truth is this: It starts getting darker from here. Each season is pregnant with the other. *You're young,* the season whispers to you tonight. *You're still so young.*

Many summers ago, when I was sixteen, I spent evenings on beaches by bonfires and all the nights were parties. One night, a beer, unopened, rolled close to the flames and sat in the sand unnoticed. The beer boiled and the pressure built and the can exploded. Razor shreds of aluminum blasted over the sand, hot shrapnel tearing across the night. A girl by the fire got hit, sliced above her lip. Blood came fast. She touched her face and looked at her fingertips covered in blood. She did not look in pain, or even afraid; more than anything she looked confused. This blood comes from me? My face? Here on this beach, on this night, by this fire? A boy pulled off his T-shirt and pressed it to her face. I can still conjure the calm in his voice as he said, "Don't worry. It's just that the face has so many blood vessels." Some people hovered around her; mostly people stood by the fire as they'd been. What could be done, after all? What had happened had happened.

But the mood around the fire tightened, quieted by the abrupt insertion of danger, of blood, of the power of the flame to hurl metal into the air and cut us all right open. "Put your face in the ocean," someone suggested. "My mom says it heals everything." We were children still, relying on our parents' prescriptions, but harm was starting to find us, there beside the fire. "Oh, thou foundling fire," says Ahab, "thou too hast thy incommunicable riddle, thy unparticipated grief."

Stardust, ocean, soil, toil, flame. The riddle we can't give words to, the grief we can't participate in, an unkept promise, a glimpse of the mystery, of the unbroken planet that may or may not have existed, the world of dew, the leap over time, there and not there. We're here and not here. Summer is made of the memory of summer. I didn't know it then, young on the sand by the fire in the night, awakening to the whole five-sensed thrill of being alive, but I sensed it at the edges, sensed IT at the edges: To forget time was to acknowledge it, winter lives in the first day of summer, the wheel of the year picks up speed as it turns. "Shall we offer the nerve-buds / of our bodies / to be nourished (or consumed) in the sun of love," poet May Swenson asks. I think the answer is yes, even though the flame will burn us to death.

Later that night on the beach, the boy sitting next to me on the driftwood log took my hand and we walked a little way from the fire and placed ourselves in the valley of a dune. The ocean crashed and siz-zled, the waves came and came and came; voices from the beach rose and fell, laughter. The fire glowed. Its warmth lived on my skin. I could not see the flames from where I was in the sand, only the tiny, orangey sparks as they rose and disappeared into the night. Only the glow, and the sense of the shadows it made. I was on my back, earth bed, star blanket. "Look at all the stars," I said, maybe not even to him. The sand was cool on my back, the earth pressing itself up into me as I was pressed into it. "Your hair smells like smoke," the boy said.

I woke up the next morning in the attic of my grandmother's house. Downstairs, on the porch, she and I watched as two people got off their bikes and went to her tangle of blackberry bushes to steal her fruit. She stood and yelled down the hill. The thieves hurried away. This is a summer memory. Summer is earth's memory. Summer is earth's memory of all the fertile formlessness, everything arriving, wet-breathed, bloodied, burning. Summer is the memory of what we know used to be, but can never wholly recall. So we remember instead: the fattest blackber-ries too high to reach, prickers that scratch the arm, catch the strap of the sundress, the berries on the bush warm, swollen, ready in the sun.

It's getting warmer. It's getting darker. Take off your clothes and slip back in.

A Last Tremble of the Wing

I HAVE MURDERED generations of fruit flies in my kitchen. They arrive in July, once the heat has settled in, and for the warmer weeks of the year, we begrudge each other's presence. I wash heads of lettuce in the sink, run a knife through fat tomatoes so they bleed on the cutting board, move a beer from fridge to freezer for ten minutes, then pour it in a glass that sweats like I do, and the fruit flies drift about for all of it. They flit about the peaches in the wooden fruit bowl on the counter of my small apartment near the river in the city. They land and rise and land on the soft down surface. I watch, wave my hand over the fruits, say, "Come on, guys, go away." They scatter, tickle the private part of my wrist, touch my skin like secrets I'm not sure I want to know. They wait a minute, land themselves on cabinet doors, wing sinkward, and then drift again back toward the sugar juice below the peachfuzz skin. They do not touch down on the onions or garlic bulbs or the hot peppers drying in the basket that hangs from the window trim. The sweet flesh pulls them. Do they suck the juice, I wonder? Lick the sweet off their—whats?—paws? fingers? feet? microscopic suction cuppers? "Go *away*," I say. They don't go away. They multiply.

Which is summer's mode. To increase, burst forth, bloom. I tell you now: I've never liked it.

How easy it is for me to get warm and stay warm in winter. How sharp and alive my mind feels in the cold. The expansiveness, the aliveness, the sinking into the meat of existence that happens when the days get dark in the afternoons. To see bare skeleton trees against the purple-blue gloam in November? Best. Give it to me all year. Summer comes and it's as though the maze ridges on the surface of my brain melt and I am left with a smoothed-out mostly useless mass of gray-pink meat-matter underneath my skull. Heat-stunned, dull, and damp with sweat or about to be. In cold, one can always put on more clothes. In thick heat, there's only so naked we can get.

I try not to fight it anymore. I embrace the sweat, the damp at my back, between my breasts, the insect tickle of a drop riding the slide between the muscles that line my spine. I surrender to having a less agile mind. A fallow period, I tell myself, use the body instead. Summer is for bodies, near naked on the shore, bare calves, thighs, shoulders.

But my body likes the cold-dark half of the year so much more, that friction, when the heat comes from the inside, when we make the heat ourselves. And so, unlike the fruit flies, unlike the rhododendrons, the honeysuckles, the peonies, the turtles, the bears, the dahlias, the daisies, the tulips, and the corn, I go dormant for a while, slink into a sort of hibernation. Let's talk again late August when we really start to notice less light and the shadows start to shift. And let's keep talking in September and October and especially in November, and then in the crystalline sobriety of January, and even February, too, longest month of the year, when the cold gray starts to weigh.

And you? What section of the year do you like best? When do you come into your fullest sense of self? What season feels like home to you? Let's loosen the boundaries, let's get unstrict with the regular definitions—summer allows for it after all, a little looser, a bit more unbound. For example, my favorite season of the year: October 13 through January 31. A little longer than the seasons we know, the deepening of late fall into early winter. That's the time that comes to my mind when we hit the summer solstice.

Because from here on, after this last long blaze of day, the days get shorter. It's chemical. I am seasonally affected. We all are. Others exist like me, ones who think of summer as something to get through, who enter into the force of their aliveness come fall.

But I don't begrudge the summer lovers, and, over time, have come to better appreciate summer's moist and verdant charms. Swimming is good. Hot dogs off the grill are good. All the colors of the petals, deep and pale. Riding a bike through the city on a warm night. Slugs leaving slick and shining trails on the sidewalks in the mornings. Open windows. Thunderstorms. It's nice to live.

Each season has its own topography, each month. "Green was the silence, wet was the light," Pablo Neruda writes in Sonnet XL, "the month of June trembled like a butterfly." June verges. It shifts. And it holds two forces at once: the start of summer, the start of darkening. Press a flowercrown upon your skull, get pressed into a bed of pine needles. Dew-moist in the morning, bodymoist on the bed. And the fruit flies seem to rise out of immaculate conception from the peach pits and the watermelon rinds and green ribbons of cucumber peel slopped together in the compost bin, so that opening the lid to dispose of more organic summer matter is to have Pandoric déjà vu, evils emerging not as ashy demons, but as tiny flies that suck sweet, mate, and die.

Summer slaughterer, I murder them. I pour old wine into a glass. A bottle of cheap white that's been rattling on the door of the fridge for months. Unfinished red gone sour and cidery in the low cabinet by the window. Pour a glassful of it, and then squeeze into the wine a stream of dish soap, which sinks like a snake to the bottom. A quick swish to move the soap around and the glass goes near the fruits in the bowl. The flies like the wine; they smell the sugar and approach the rim. It's irresistible. They're drawn by the promise of a sweet feed without end. They hover and land on the lip. Then they dive in. One, another, another. The slick of the soap, it alters the surface tension of the wine in the glass, so that, once in, once they touch, there is no lifting up and out again. They soak on the surface, and then they sink, absorbed into this countertop abyss. Dropping drunk, they drown.

Their bodies collect at the bottom like the flecked dregs of a torn teabag and I pour them down the sink drain with a pang. Lives, after all. Small lives, gone and done, and a soapy boozy smell rises from the drain.

More will come. And more again. As long as it's warm. As long as summer continues to ripen life, firm to sweet to rot. And I like to think it's a nice end for them, of all possible ends. Loose, warm, wet, a tipsy grin, a last tremble of the wing. A summer fate. A sweet smell, a plunge, fast as that, and then the dark.

Plant Matter

The following are the plants and herbs most strongly linked with the summer solstice. They're woven into flower crowns, tossed into flames, hung on doorways, made into tinctures and teas. On the solstice, when the sun's at its peak and the light hits the earth more directly than on any other day of the year, the plants, the herbs in particular, are said to be possessed of a different power, at the peak of their potency. Besides those below, other plants with strong links to the summer solstice include fennel, hemp, rosemary, sage, mint, elder, chamomile, roses, thyme, and meadowsweet.

St. John's Wort

Little buttercuppy flowers on the bush, five petals spread like open arms, a gesture of unalloyed welcome, total embrace. I'm here! Now! For all of it! From the center, fine yellow wands splay up and out like rays of sun, feelers reaching out to touch what is. It's the plant most strongly associated with the summer solstice, and its sunshiny disposition is said to help burn away the distorting fog of depression. A sorrow sweeper, it aims itself at other ailments, too, shingles, rheumatism; it helps heal burns and wounds. It's a plant that bleeds itself: Pinch the leaves or the buds and you stain your fingertips dark red. People flung it into midsummer fires for ongoing good health and fertility in humans and livestock alike, and hung it on lintels to protect against storm and harm. It's likewise linked with future-seeing in the realms of romance and longevity. In Celtic cultures, it was hung over the beds in a household; the next morning, whoever's was most wilted would be the first to die. It's also powerful enough to bully other medications, like birth control, for one example; take care with how you use it.

Lavender

In delicate swaying rises—stalks too tough a word— the gentle purple flowerettes exhale their fresh and cleansing breath. The color mixes blue and gray and purple, and in that way, like the sky during moments in the in-betweens, early morning, dusk. A scent for soap, it's an antiseptic, on clothes and skin, and it's said to wash away worries as well, calming the mind of its agitations and nerves. The smell, bath towels off the line; sheets that have hung in sun and dried; light filtering into a room through a thin linen curtain when the day is getting warmer; a bar of soap velvety between the palms that sits on a dish at your grandmother's. Breathe in, it whispers, nature gives us this.

Vervain

Scentless vervain with so many nicknames: simpler's joy, Juno's tears, pigeonweed, holy herb, enchanter's plant. It's said that vervain grew where the tears of Isis landed as she wept over the death of Osiris. It's said that vervain was used to staunch Christ's wounds on the cross. It's believed to banish kidney stones, as well as soothe aches and insomnia and urinary tract infections. The tiny flowers, blue or white, grow in small spiking clustered bunches on knee-high to waist-high stems. A staple of the flower crown across time and culture, it served as love charm, too. In his *Eclogues*, Virgil writes of using it to bewitch a love. "Burn thereon rich vervain and the strength of frankincense, so I may seek by magic rites to turn my love's sound mind."

Calendula

It sounds like the name you might give a pet cloud. It's an edible flower, and its sunsetty petals added to salads, eggs, and stews were a "comforter of the heart and spirits" and used "to expel any malignant or pestilential quality which might annoy," according to Nicholas Culpeper, who compiled *Culpeper's*

Complete Herbal in 1653. Like many of the other herbs and flowers of the solstice, it's an anti-inflammatory, antibacterial, antifungal. It's a vulnerary (speeds the healing of your wounds), an emmenagogue (stimulates your menstrual flow), and a lymphagogue (sets your lymphatic system into action). On your skin, use it for bug bites, bruises, eczema, to soothe cracked nipples, stings, or burns.

Mugwort

Into big barrels of midsummer beer went the mugwort, brewed for the parties that went the whole night. It's bushy and abundant, and better yet, it opens doors, allows one into pockets of one's mind that one doesn't always have access to, especially in the dreamlife realm, where it's believed that mugwort provides a greater clarity of vision and insight. Tuck some in a pouch, tuck it under a pillow, tuck yourself in, see where you go. It makes things vivid. It's a protector, too. St. John the Baptist was said to have worn a belt of it to ward off evil. At midsummer, it keeps the demons away, and all manner of evil forces.

Yarrow

Chiron was a centaur, wisest of them all. A healer, he was wounded by Hercules accidentally and flung into the sky as a series of stars, our constellation

Sagittarius. Before he got sent starward, he mentored young Achilles, taught the warrior what he knew of how to heal with flowers and with herbs. Like yarrow, with its bitter taste, known as *Achillea millefolium*. *Achillea* for Achilles, *millefolium* for a thousand flowers, the way they collect in fleecy lacy canopies, so many tiny flowers all together. Yellow, white, or red. The benefits seem endless: anti-inflammatory, antibacterial, antispasmodic, a depurative (detoxifier), a febrifuge (makes your fever flee), a nervine (it acts on your nervous system). It was also known as nosebleed; it encourages blood clotting. It disinfects cuts and scrapes; in tea, it helps you sweat your flu away, or slows heavy menstrual bleeding. Yarrow under the pillow, dream of your true love. In *The Iliad*, a moment of injury, an arrow in the thigh. Patroculus, taught by Achilles, taught by Chiron, "washed the black blood running from it . . . and laid on a bitter root to make pain disappear, one which stayed all kinds of pain. And the wound dried, and the flow of blood stopped." On my desk, a spray of yarrow, dried now, dusty yellow, sits in an old honey jar. Soothe my wounds. Tell me who I love.

Works Cited

Anne Carson, *Plainwater* (Vintage Contemporaries, 2000).

Inger Christensen, *it*, translated by Susanna Nied
(Gyldendal, 1969 / New Directions, 2006).

Nicholas Culpeper, *Culpeper's Complete Herbal* (1653).

James Frazer, *The Golden Bough: A Study in Magic and
Religion* (Macmillan, 1890).

Robert Graves, *The White Goddess* (Faber & Faber, 1948).

Nathaniel Hawthorne, "The May-Pole of Merry Mount,"
from *Twice-Told Tales* (American Stationers Co./John
B. Russell, 1837).

Tony Hoagland, "Jet," from *Donkey Gospel* (Graywolf
Press, 1998).

Homer, *The Iliad*, translated by Stanley Lombardo
(Hackett, 1997).

Kobayashi Issa, "World of Dew," from *The Essential
Haiku: Versions of Basho, Buson & Issa*, translated and
edited by Robert Hass (Ecco Press, 1995).

Tove Jansson, *The Summer Book*, translated by Thomas
Teal (Albert Bonniers Förlag, 1972 / Pantheon Books,
1974).

Janis Joplin, "Summertime," lyrics by George Gershwin,
Ira Gershwin, DuBose Heyward, from *Cheap Thrills,*
by Big Brother and the Holding Company (Columbia
Records, 1968).

James Joyce, *Finnegans Wake* (The Viking Press, 1939).

Heidi Julavits, from "How I Learned to Love Almost Dying," from *The Cut*, September 23, 2015.

D. H. Lawrence, *Studies in Classic American Literature* (Thomas Seltzer, 1923).

Herman Melville, *Moby-Dick or, The Whale* (Richard Bentley, 1851).

Aimee Nezhukumatathil, "Summer Haibun," from *Oceanic* (Copper Canyon Press, 2018).

Octavio Paz, "Sunstone," from *The Collected Poems of Octavio Paz: 1957–1987*, edited by Eliot Weinberger (New Directions, 1987).

M. C. Richards, *Centering in Pottery, Poetry, and the Person* (Wesleyan University Press, 1964).

May Swenson, "Swimmers," from *The Complete Love Poems of May Swenson* (Mariner Books, 2003).

Virgil, *The Eclogues*, translated by John William Mackail (George Pulman & Sons, 1908).

Virginia Woolf, *The Waves* (Hogarth Press, 1931).

Led Zeppelin, "Stairway to Heaven," from *Led Zeppelin IV* (Atlantic Records, 1971).

Acknowledgments

Working with editor Nadja Spiegelman on these and other essays for *The Paris Review Daily* has been one of the highlights of my writing life; deepest thanks to her. Thank you to Joshua Bodwell and all of Black Sparrow Press and David R. Godine. Thank you to Gillian MacKenzie, again and again, as well as to Kirsten Wolf. Thank you to Jennifer Muller for the beautiful honeycomb cover. Thank you to Will, Sam, my parents, Pam, Jenny, Alicia, Sharon, John, Shuchi, Kim, and Lisa.

Text set in Bembo with Mrs. Eaves for titling. Interior design and composition by Brooke Koven. Cover design by Jennifer Muller.

Black Sparrow Press was founded by John and Barbara Martin in 1966 and continued by them until 2002. The iconic sparrow logo was drawn by Barbara Martin.